FARM CHARM

In the ORCHARD

by Pearl Markovics

Consultant:
Beth Gambro
Reading Specialist
Yorkville, Illinois

Contents

BEARPORT PUBLISHING

New York, New York

In the Orchard

Look around.

What do you see?

I see trees in the orchard.

What do you see?

I see flowers
in the orchard.

What do you see?

I see bees in the orchard.

Bzzz, bzzz.

What do you see?

I see birds in the orchard.

Chirp!

What do you see?

I see apples in
the orchard.

Yum!

Look closely!

What do you see in the orchard?

Key Words

apples

bees

birds

flowers

trees

Index

About the Author

Pearl Markovics grew up on a small farm in New York. She enjoys picking ripe, juicy peaches during the summer.